THE INTERNATIONAL PSYCHO-ANALYTICAL LIBRARY
EDITED BY ERNEST JONES
No. 12.

THE EGO AND THE ID

BY

SIGM. FREUD, M.D., LL.D.

AUTHORIZED TRANSLATION
BY
JOAN RIVIERE

Martino Publishing
Mansfield Centre, CT
2011

Martino Publishing
P.O. Box 373,
Mansfield Centre, CT 06250 USA

ISBN 1-891396-81-1

© *2011 Martino Publishing*

Cover design by T. Matarazzo

Printed in the United States of America On 100% Acid-Free Paper

THE INTERNATIONAL PSYCHO-ANALYTICAL LIBRARY
EDITED BY ERNEST JONES
No. 12.

THE EGO AND THE ID

BY

SIGM. FREUD, M.D., LL.D.

AUTHORIZED TRANSLATION
BY
JOAN RIVIERE

PUBLISHED BY THE HOGARTH PRESS, 37 MECKLENBURGH
SQUARE, LONDON, AND THE INSTITUTE OF PSYCHO-
ANALYSIS
1927

Published by the Hogarth Press
1927

CONTENTS

TRANSLATOR'S NOTE

DAS *Ich und das Es* was published in 1923 by the Internationaler Psycho-analytischer Verlag, Vienna. I was able to discuss the translation of this very obscure book with the Author, and became responsible for it, so that it bears my name. The actual version which follows, however, though drafted by me, has been worked over by three people. Dr. Ernest Jones as Editor has given it his usual care; Fräulein Anna Freud has corrected mis-apprehensions and also referred to the Author several doubts that arose; but if the trans-lation attains any exactness in rendering the Author's thoughts and intentions, this is almost wholly due to Mr. James Strachey's sedulous and discriminating exertions in aid of clear eluci-dation of the text.

J. R.

INTRODUCTION

IN my essay, *Beyond the Pleasure Principle*, published in 1920,[1] I began the discussion of a train of thought, my personal attitude towards which, as I mentioned there, might be described as a sort of benevolent curiosity; in the following pages this train of thought is developed further. I have taken up those ideas and brought them into connection with various facts observed in psycho-analysis and have endeavoured to draw fresh conclusions from the combination; in the present work, however, no further contributions are levied from biology, and it consequently stands in a closer relation to psycho-analysis than does *Beyond the Pleasure Principle*. The thoughts contained in it are synthetic rather than speculative in character and their aim appears to be an ambitious one. I am aware, however, that they do not go beyond the baldest outlines and I am

[1] *Beyond the Pleasure Principle*, London, 1922; translated from *Jenseits des Lustprinzips*, Vienna, 1920.

perfectly content to recognize their limitations in
this respect.

At the same time, the train of thought touches
upon things not hitherto dealt with in the work
psycho-analysis has done, and it cannot avoid concerning itself with a number of theories propounded
by non-analysts or by former analysts on their
retreat from analysis.   I am as a rule always ready
to acknowledge my debts to other workers, but on
this occasion I feel myself under no such obliga-
tion.   If there are certain things to which hitherto
psycho-analysis has not given adequate consideration, that is not because it has overlooked their
effects or wished to deny their significance, but
because it pursues a particular path which had not
yet carried it so far.   And, moreover, now that
these things have at last been overtaken, they
appear to psycho-analysis in a different shape from
that in which they appear to the other people.

I

CONSCIOUSNESS AND THE UNCONSCIOUS

I N this preliminary chapter there is nothing new to be said and it will not be possible to avoid repeating what has often been said before.

The division of mental life into what is conscious and what is unconscious is the fundamental premise on which psycho-analysis is based ; and this division alone makes it possible for it to understand pathological mental processes, which are as common as they are important, and to co-ordinate them scientifically. Stated once more in a different way : psycho-analysis cannot accept the view that consciousness is the essence of mental life, but is obliged to regard consciousness as one property of mental life, which may co-exist along with its other properties or may be absent.

If I were to allow myself to suppose that every one interested in psychology would read this book, I should still be prepared to find that some of them would stop short even at this point and go no further ; for here we have the first shibboleth of psycho-analysis.   To most people who have had a philosophical education the idea of anything mental which is not also conscious is so inconceivable that it seems to them absurd and refutable simply by logic.   I believe this is only because they have never studied the mental phenomena of hypnosis and dreams, which—quite apart from pathological manifestations—necessitate this conclusion.   Thus their psychology of consciousness is incapable of solving the problems of dreams and hypnosis.

The term ' conscious ' is, to start with, a purely descriptive one, resting on a perception of the most direct and certain character.   Experience shows, next, that a mental element (for instance, an idea) is not as a rule permanently conscious. On the contrary, a state of consciousness is characteristically very transitory ;   an idea that is conscious now is no longer so a moment later, although it can become so again under certain conditions that are easily brought about.   What the idea was in the interval we do not know.   We can say that it was *latent*, and by this we mean that it was *capable of becoming conscious* at any time.   Or, if we say that it was *unconscious*, we are

giving an equally correct description.   Thus ' unconscious ' in this sense of the word coincides with
' latent and capable of becoming conscious '.   The
philosophers would no doubt object : ' No, the
term unconscious does not apply here ; so long as
the idea was in a state of latency it was not a
mental element at all '.   To contradict them at
this point would lead to nothing more profitable
than a war of words.

But we have arrived at the term or concept
of ' unconscious ' along another path, by taking
account of certain experiences in which mental
dynamics play a part.   We have found, that is, we
have been obliged to assume, that very powerful
mental processes or ideas exist—here a quantitative or *economic* factor comes into question for the
first time—which can produce in the mind all the
effects that ordinary ideas do (including effects
that can in their turn become conscious as ideas)
without themselves becoming conscious.   It is
unnecessary here to repeat in detail what has been
explained so often before.   We need only say that
this is the point at which psycho-analytic theory
steps in—with the assertion that such ideas cannot
become conscious because a certain force is opposed
to them, that otherwise they could become conscious, and that then one would see how little they

differ from other elements which are admittedly mental. The fact that in the technique of psycho-analysis a means has been found by which the opposing force can be removed and the ideas in question made conscious renders this theory irrefutable. The state in which the ideas existed before being made conscious is called by us *repression*, and we assert that the force which instituted the repression and maintains it is perceived as *resistance* during the work of analysis.

We obtain our concept of the unconscious, therefore, from the theory of repression. The repressed serves us as a prototype of the unconscious. We see, however, that we have two kinds of unconscious—that which is latent but capable of becoming conscious, and that which is repressed and not capable of becoming conscious in the ordinary way. This piece of insight into mental dynamics cannot fail to affect terminology and description. That which is latent, and only unconscious in the descriptive and not in the dynamic sense, we call *preconscious* ; the term unconscious we reserve for the dynamically unconscious repressed, so that we now have three terms, conscious (Cs), preconscious (Pcs), and unconscious (Ucs), which are no longer purely descriptive in sense. The Pcs is presumably a great deal closer

to the Cs than is the Ucs, and since we have called
the Ucs mental we shall with even less hesitation
call the latent Pcs mental. But why do we not
choose, instead of this, to remain in agreement
with the philosophers and, in a consistent way, to
distinguish the Pcs as well as the Ucs from what is
conscious in the mind ? The philosophers would
propose that both the Pcs and the Ucs should be
described as two varieties or levels of ' psychoid ',
and harmony would be established. But endless
difficulties in exposition would follow ; and the
one important fact, that the two kinds of ' psychoid ' as thus defined coincide in almost every
other respect with what is admittedly mental,
would be forced into the background in the interests
of a prejudice dating from a period in which they,
or the most important part of them, were still
unknown.

We can now set to work comfortably with our
three terms, Cs, Pcs, and Ucs, so long as we do not
forget that, while in the descriptive sense there are
two kinds of unconscious, in the dynamic sense
there is only one. For purposes of exposition this
distinction can in many cases be ignored, but in
others it is of course indispensable. At the same
time, we have become more or less accustomed to
these two meanings of the term unconscious and

have managed pretty well with them.   As far as I can see, it is impossible to avoid this ambiguity; the distinction between conscious and unconscious is in the last resort a question of a perception which must be either affirmed or denied, and the act of perception itself tells us nothing of the reason why a thing is or is not perceived.   No one has a right to complain because the actual phenomenon expresses the underlying dynamic factors ambiguously.[1]

[1] This may be compared with my ' Note on the Unconscious in Psycho-Analysis' (1912), *Collected Papers*, vol. iv.   A new turn taken by criticisms of the unconscious deserves consideration at this point.   Many investigators, who do not refuse to recognize the facts of psycho-analysis but who are unwilling to accept the unconscious, find a way out of the difficulty in the fact, which no one contests, that in consciousness (regarded as a phenomenon) it is possible to distinguish a great variety of gradations in intensity or clarity.   Just as there are ideas which are very vividly, keenly, and definitely conscious, so we also entertain others which are but faintly, hardly even noticeably conscious ; those that are most faintly conscious are, it is argued, the ones to which psycho-analysis wishes to apply the unsuitable name unconscious.   These, however (the argument proceeds), are also conscious or ' in consciousness ' just as much as the others, and can be made fully and intensely conscious if sufficient attention is paid to them.

In so far as it is possible to influence by arguments the decision of a question of this kind which is based either on a convention or on emotional factors, we may make the following comments.   The reference to gradations of clarity in consciousness is in no way conclusive and has no more evidential value than such analogous statements as : ' There are so many gradations in illumination—from the brightest and most dazzling light to the dimmest glimmer—that we may conclude that there is no such thing as darkness at all ' ; or, ' There are varying degrees

In the further course of psycho-analytic work, however, even these distinctions have proved to be inadequate and, for practical purposes, insufficient. This has become clear in more ways than one ; but the decisive instance is as follows. We have formulated the idea that in every individual there is a coherent organization of mental processes, which we call his *ego*. This ego includes consciousness and it controls the approaches to motility, *i.e.* to the discharge of excitations into

---

of vitality, consequently there is no such thing as death '. Such statements may in a certain sense have a meaning, but for practical purposes they are worthless. This will be seen if one proceeds to draw certain conclusions from them, such as, ' it is not necessary, therefore, to strike a light ', or, ' therefore all living things are immortal '. Further, to include ' what is unnoticeable ' under the concept of ' what is conscious ' is simply to play havoc with the one and only piece of direct and certain knowledge that we have about the mind. And after all, a consciousness of which one knows nothing seems to me a good deal more absurd than an unconscious mind. Finally, this attempt to equate what is unnoticed with what is unconscious is obviously made without taking into account the dynamic conditions involved, which were the decisive factors in formulating the psycho-analytic view. For it ignores two facts : first, that it is exceedingly difficult and requires very great effort to concentrate enough attention on something unnoticed of this kind ; and secondly, that when this has been achieved the thought which was previously unnoticed is not recognized by consciousness, but often seems utterly alien and opposed to it and is promptly disavowed by it. Escaping from the unconscious in this way and taking refuge in what is scarcely noticed or unnoticed is, therefore, after all only an expression of the preconceived belief which regards the identity of mental and conscious as settled once and for all.

the external world; it is this institution in the mind which regulates all its own constituent processes, and which goes to sleep at night, though even then it continues to exercise a censorship upon dreams. From this ego proceed the repressions, too, by means of which an attempt is made to cut off certain trends in the mind not merely from consciousness but also from their other forms of manifestation and activity. In analysis these trends which have been shut out stand in opposition to the ego and the analysis is faced with the task of removing the resistances which the ego displays against concerning itself with the repressed. Now we find that during analysis, when we put certain tasks before the patient, he gets into difficulties; his associations fail when they ought to be getting near to the repressed. We then tell him that he is dominated by a resistance; but he is quite unaware of the fact, and, even if he guesses from his feelings of discomfort that a resistance is now at work in him, he does not know what it is nor how to describe it. Since, however, there can be no question but that this resistance emanates from his ego and belongs to it, we find ourselves in an unforeseen situation. We have come upon something in the ego itself which is also unconscious, which behaves exactly like the repressed, that is, which produces powerful effects without itself being conscious and which requires special work before it can be made conscious. From the point of view of analytic practice, the consequence of this piece of observation is that we land in endless confusion and difficulty if we cling to our former way of expressing ourselves and try, for instance, to derive neuroses from a conflict between the conscious and the unconscious. We shall have to substitute for this antithesis another, taken from our understanding of the structural conditions of the mind, namely, the antithesis between the organized ego and what is repressed and dissociated from it.[1]

For our conception of the unconscious, however, the consequences of our new observation are even more important. Dynamic considerations caused us to make our first correction ; our knowledge of the structure of the mind leads to the second. We recognize that the Ucs does not coincide with what is repressed ; it is still true that all that is repressed is Ucs, but not that the whole Ucs is repressed. A part of the ego, too—and Heaven knows how important a part—may be Ucs, undoubtedly is Ucs. And this Ucs belonging to the ego is not latent like the Pcs ; for if it were, it could not be

[1] Cf. *Beyond the Pleasure Principle*.

B

activated without becoming Cs, and the process of making it conscious would not encounter such great difficulties. When we find ourselves thus confronted by the necessity of postulating a third Ucs which is not repressed, we must admit that the property of being unconscious begins to lose significance for us. It becomes a quality which can have many implications, so that we are unable to make it, as we should have hoped to do, the basis of far-reaching and inevitable conclusions. Nevertheless, we must beware of ignoring this property, for in the last resort the quality of being conscious or not is the single ray of light that penetrates the obscurity of depth-psychology.

II

THE EGO AND THE ID

PATHOLOGICAL research has centred our
interest too exclusively on the repressed.
We wish to know more about the ego,
now that we know that it, too, can be unconscious in the proper sense of the word. Hitherto
the only guide we have had while pursuing our
investigations has been the distinguishing mark
of being conscious or unconscious; and in the
end we have come to see that this quality itself
is ambiguous.

Now all our knowledge is invariably bound up
with consciousness. Even knowledge of the Ucs
can only be obtained by making it conscious. But
stop, how is that possible? What does it mean
when we say 'making it conscious'? How can
that come about?

We already know the point from which we have
to start in this connection. We have said that
consciousness is the *superficies* of the mental

apparatus; that is, we have allocated it as a function to the system which is situated nearest to the external world.   Incidentally, on this occasion the topographical terminology does not merely serve to describe the nature of the function, but actually corresponds to the anatomical facts.[1]   Our investigations too must take this surface organ of perception as a starting-point.

All perceptions which are received from without (sense-perceptions) and from within—what we call sensations and feelings—are Cs from the start. But how is it with those internal processes which we may—vaguely and inexactly—sum up under the name of thought-processes ?   They represent displacements of mental energy which are effected somewhere in the interior of the apparatus as this energy proceeds on its way towards action.   Do they advance towards the superficies, which then allows of the development of consciousness ?   Or does consciousness make its way towards them ? This is clearly one of the difficulties that spring up when one begins to take the spatial or ‘ topographical ’ conception of mental life seriously. Both these possibilities are equally unïmaginable ; there must be a third contingency to meet the case.

[1] *Beyond the Pleasure Principle.*

I have already, in another place,[1] suggested that the real difference between a Ucs and a Pcs idea (thought) consists in this : that the former is worked out upon some sort of material which remains unrecognized, whereas the latter (the Pcs) has in addition been brought into connection with verbal images.   This is the first attempt to find a distinguishing mark for the two systems, the Pcs and the Ucs, other than their relation to consciousness.   It would seem, then, that the question, ' How does a thing become conscious ? ' could be put more advantageously thus : ' How does a thing become preconscious ? '   And the answer would be : ' By coming into connection with the verbal images that correspond to it '.

These verbal images are memory-residues ; they were at one time perceptions, and like all memory-residues they can become conscious again.   Before we concern ourselves further with their nature, it dawns upon us like a new discovery that only something which has once been a Cs perception can become conscious, and that anything arising from within (apart from feelings) that seeks to become conscious must try to transform itself into external perceptions : this can be done by way of memory-traces.

[1] ' The Unconscious ' (1915), *Collected Papers*, vol. iv.

We conceive of memory-residues as contained in systems which are directly adjacent to the system Pcpt-Cs, so that the cathexes pertaining to the memory-residues can readily extend outward on to the elements of the latter system. We are immediately reminded of hallucinations here, and of the fact that the most vivid memory is always distinguishable both from a hallucination and from an external perception ; but it will also occur to us that when a memory is revived the cathexis in the memory-system will remain in force, whereas a hallucination which is not distinguishable from a perception can arise when the cathexis does not merely extend over from the memory-trace to the Pcpt-element, but passes over to it entirely.

Verbal residues are derived primarily from auditory perceptions, so that the system Pcs has, as it were, a special sensory source. The visual components of verbal images are secondary, acquired through reading, and may to begin with be left on one side ; so may the sensori-motor images of words, which, except with deaf-mutes, play an auxiliary part. The essence of a word is after all the memory-trace of a word that has been heard.

We must not be led away, in the interests of simplification perhaps, into forgetting the importance of optical memory-residues—those of *things* (as opposed to *words*)—or to deny that it is possible for thought-processes to become conscious through a reversion to visual residues, and that in many people this seems to be a favourite method. The study of dreams and of preconscious phantasies on the lines of J. Varendonck's observations gives us an idea of the special character of this visual thinking. We learn that what becomes conscious is as a rule only the concrete subject-matter of the thought, and that the relations between the various elements of this subject-matter, which is what specially characterizes thought, cannot be given visual expression. Thinking in pictures is, therefore, only a very incomplete form of becoming conscious. In some way, too, it approximates more closely to unconscious processes than does thinking in words, and it is unquestionably older than the latter both ontogenetically and phylogenetically.

To return to our argument : if, therefore, this is the way in which something that is in itself unconscious becomes preconscious, the question how something that is repressed can be made (pre)conscious would be answered as follows. It is done by supplying through the work of the analysis Pcs connecting-links of the kind we have been discussing. Consciousness remains where it is, therefore ; but, on the other hand, the Ucs does not rise up into the Cs.

Whereas the relation between external perceptions and the ego is quite perspicuous, that between internal perceptions and the ego requires special investigation. It gives rise once more to a doubt whether we are really justified in referring the whole of consciousness to the single superficial system Pcpt-Cs.

Internal perceptions yield sensations of processes arising in the most diverse and certainly also in the deepest strata of the mental apparatus. Very little is known about these sensations and feelings ; the best examples we have of them are still those belonging to the pleasure-pain series. They are more fundamental, more elementary, than perceptions arising externally and they can come into being even when consciousness is clouded. I have elsewhere expressed my views about their great economic significance and its metapsychological foundation. These sensations are multilocular, like external perceptions ; they may come from different places simultaneously and may thus have different or even opposite qualities.

Sensations of a pleasurable nature are not characterized by any inherently impelling quality, whereas 'painful' ones possess this quality in a high degree. The latter impel towards change, towards discharge, and that is why we interpret 'pain' as implying a heightening and pleasure a lowering of energic cathexis. Suppose we describe what becomes conscious in the shape of pleasure and 'pain' as an undetermined quantitative and qualitative element in the mind; the question then is whether that element can become conscious where it actually is, or whether it must first be transmitted into the system Pcpt.

Clinical experience decides for the latter. It shows us that this undetermined element behaves like a repressed impulse. It can exert driving force without the ego noticing the compulsion. Not until there is resistance to the compulsion, and blocking of the discharge-reaction, does the undetermined element instantly become conscious as 'pain'. In the same way that tensions arising from physical need can remain unconscious, so also can physical pain—a thing intermediate between external and internal perception, which acts like an internal perception even when its source is in the external world. It remains true again, therefore, that sensations and feelings only become conscious through reaching the system Pcpt; if the way forward is barred, they do not come into being as sensations, although the undetermined element corresponding to them is the same as if they did.   We then come to speak, in a condensed and not entirely correct manner, of ' unconscious feelings ', keeping up an analogy with unconscious ideas which is not altogether justifiable.   Actually the difference is that, whereas with Ucs *ideas* connecting-links must be forged before they can be brought into the Cs, with *feelings*, which are themselves transmitted directly, there is no necessity for this.   In other words : the distinction between Cs and Pcs has no meaning where feelings are concerned ; the Pcs here falls out of account, and feelings are either conscious or unconscious. Even when they are connected with verbal images, their becoming conscious is not due to that circumstance, but they become so directly.

The part played by verbal images now becomes perfectly clear.   By their interposition internal thought-processes are made into perceptions.   It is like a demonstration of the theorem that all knowledge has its origin in external perception. It may sometimes happen that a hyper-cathexis of the process of thinking takes place, in which case thoughts are *perceived* in the literal sense of the word—as if they came from without—and are consequently held to be true.

After this clarifying of the relations between external and internal perception and the superficial system Pcpt-Cs, we can go on to work out our conception of the ego.   It clearly starts out from its nucleus, the system Pcpt, and begins by embracing the Pcs, which is adjacent to the memory-residues.   But the ego, as we have learnt, is also unconscious.

Now I think we shall gain a great deal by following the suggestion of a writer who, from personal motives, vainly insists that he has nothing to do with the rigours of pure science.   I am speaking of Georg Groddeck, who is never tired of pointing out that the conduct through life of what we call our ego is essentially passive, and that, as he expresses it, we are 'lived' by unknown and uncontrollable forces.[1]   We have all had impressions of the same kind, even though they may not have overwhelmed us to the exclusion of all others, and we need feel no hesitation in finding a place for Groddeck's discovery in the fabric of science. I propose to take it into account by calling the entity which starts out from the system Pcpt and begins by being Pcs the ego, and by following Groddeck in giving to the other part of the mind, into which this entity extends and which

[1] G. Groddeck, *Das Buch vom Es*, Vienna, 1923.

behaves as though it were Ucs, the name of
Id (Es).[1]

We shall soon see whether this conception
affords us any gain in understanding or any advantage for purposes of description. We shall now
look upon the mind of an individual as an unknown
and unconscious id, upon whose surface rests the
ego, developed from its nucleus the Pcpt-system.
If we make an effort to conceive of this pictorially,
we may add that the ego does not envelop the
whole of the id, but only does so to the extent to
which the system Pcpt forms its surface, more or
less as the germinal layer rests upon the ovum.
The ego is not sharply separated from the id ; its
lower portion merges into it.

But the repressed merges into the id as well,
and is simply a part of it. The repressed is only
cut off sharply from the ego by the resistances of
repression ; it can communicate with the ego
through the id. We at once realize that almost all
the delimitations we have been led into outlining
by our study of pathology relate only to the

[1] Groddeck himself no doubt followed the example of Nietzsche,
who habitually used this grammatical term for whatever in our
nature is impersonal and, so to speak, subject to natural law.

[For the German ' *Es* ', which means literally ' it ', the corresponding Latin word ' id ' has been adopted on the analogy of
' ego ' which is the accepted rendering of the German ' *Ich* '
(literally ' I ').—TRANS.]

superficial levels of the mental apparatus—the only ones known to us. The state of things which we have been describing can be represented diagrammatically (Fig. 1); though it must be remarked that the form chosen has no pretensions to any special applicability, but is merely intended to serve for purposes of exposition. We might add,

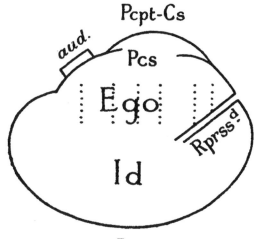

FIG. 1.

perhaps, that the ego wears an auditory lobe—on one side only, as we learn from cerebral anatomy. It wears it crooked, as one might say.

It is easy to see that the ego is that part of the id which has been modified by the direct influence of the external world acting through the Pcpt-Cs: in a sense it is an extension of the surface-differentiation. Moreover, the ego has the task of

bringing the influence of the external world to
bear upon the id and its tendencies, and endeavours
to substitute the reality-principle for the pleasure-
principle which reigns supreme in the id.   In the
ego perception plays the part which in the id
devolves upon instinct.   The ego represents what
we call reason and sanity, in contrast to the id
which contains the passions.   All this falls into line
with popular distinctions which we are all familiar
with ; at the same time, however, it is only to be
regarded as holding good in an average or ' ideal '
case.

   The functional importance of the ego is mani-
fested in the fact that normally control over the
approaches to motility devolves upon it.   Thus in
its relation to the id it is like a man on horseback,
who has to hold in check the superior strength of
the horse ; with this difference, that the rider
seeks to do so with his own strength while the ego
uses borrowed forces.   The illustration may be
carried further.   Often a rider, if he is not to be
parted from his horse, is obliged to guide it where
it wants to go; so in the same way the ego constantly carries into action the wishes of the id as if
they were its own.

   It seems that another factor, besides the influence of the system Pcpt, has been at work in

bringing about the formation of the ego and its differentiation from the id. The body itself, and above all its surface, is a place from which both external and internal perceptions may spring. It is seen in the same way as any other object, but to the touch it yields two kinds of sensations, one of which is equivalent to an internal perception. Psychophysiology has fully discussed the manner in which the body attains its special position among other objects in the world of perception. Pain seems also to play a part in the process, and the way in which we gain new knowledge of our organs during painful illnesses is perhaps a prototype of the way by which in general we arrive at the idea of our own body.

The ego is first and foremost a body-ego ; it is not merely a surface entity, but it is itself the projection of a surface.[1] If we wish to find an anatomical analogy for it we can easily identify it with the ' cortical homunculus ' of the anatomists, which stands on its head in the cortex, sticks its heels into the air, faces backwards and, as we know, has its speech-area on the left-hand side.

    [1] [*I.e.* the ego is ultimately derived from bodily sensations, chiefly from those springing from the surface of the body. It may thus be regarded as a mental projection of the surface of the body, besides, as we have seen above, representing the superficies of the mental apparatus.—Authorized note by the Translator.]

The relation of the ego to consciousness has been gone into repeatedly; yet there are still some important facts in this connection which remain to be described. Accustomed as we are to taking our social or ethical standard of values along with us wherever we go, we feel no surprise at hearing that the scene of the activities of the lower passions is in the unconscious; we expect, moreover, that the higher any mental function ranks in our scale of values the more easily it will find access to consciousness assured to it. Here, however, psycho-analytic experience disappoints us. On the one hand, we have evidence that even subtle and intricate intellectual operations which ordinarily require strenuous concentration can equally be carried out preconsciously and without coming into consciousness. Instances of this are quite incontestable; they may occur, for instance, during sleep, as is shown when some one finds, immediately after waking, that he knows the solution of a difficult mathematical or other problem with which he had been wrestling in vain the day before.[1]

There is another phenomenon, however, which is far stranger. In our analyses we discover that there are people in whom the faculties of self-

[1] I was quite recently told an instance of this which was, in fact, brought up as an objection against my description of the ' dream-work '.

criticism and conscience—mental activities, that is, that rank as exceptionally high ones—are unconscious and unconsciously produce effects of the greatest importance ; the example of resistances remaining unconscious during analysis is therefore by no means unique. But this new discovery, which compels us, in spite of our critical faculties, to speak of an ' unconscious sense of guilt ', bewilders us far more than the other and sets us fresh problems, especially when we gradually come to see that in a great number of neuroses this unconscious sense of guilt plays a decisive economic part and puts the most powerful obstacles in the way of recovery. If we come back once more to our scale of values, we shall have to say that not only what is lowest but also what is highest in the ego can be unconscious. It is as if we were thus supplied with a proof of what we have just asserted of the conscious ego : that it is first and foremost a body-ego.

III

THE EGO AND THE SUPER-EGO
(EGO-IDEAL)

I F the ego were merely the part of the id that is modified by the influence of the perceptual system, the representative in the mind of the real external world, we should have a simple state of things to deal with. But there is a further complication.

The considerations that led us to assume the existence of a differentiating grade within the ego, which may be called the ego-ideal or super-ego, have been set forth elsewhere.[1] They still hold good.[2] The new proposition which must now be

[1] 'On Narcissism : an Introduction' (1914), Collected Papers, vol. iv. ; and Group Psychology and the Analysis of the Ego (1921), London, 1922.

[2] Except that I seem to have been mistaken in ascribing the function of testing the reality of things to this super-ego—a point which needs correction. The view that the testing of reality is rather one of the functions of the ego itself would fit in perfectly with what we know of the relations of the ego to the world of perception. Some earlier suggestions about a 'nucleus of the ego', never very definitely formulated, also require to be put

gone into is that this part of the ego is less closely connected with consciousness than the rest.

At this point we must widen our range a little. We succeeded in explaining the painful disorder of melancholia by supposing that, in those suffering from it, an object which was lost has been re-instated within the ego ; that is, that an object-cathexis has been replaced by an identification.[1] When this explanation was first proposed, how-ever, we did not appreciate the full significance of the process and did not know how common and how typical it is. Since then we have come to under-stand that this kind of substitution has a great share in determining the form taken on by the ego and that it contributes materially towards building up what is called its ' character '.

At the very beginning, in the primitive oral phase of the individual's existence, object-cathexis and identification are hardly to be distinguished from each other. We can only suppose that later on object-cathexes proceed from the id, in which erotic trends are felt as needs. The ego, which at its inception is still far from robust, becomes aware of the object-cathexes, and either acquiesces in

---

right, since the system Pcpt-Cs alone can be regarded as the nucleus of the ego.

[1] ' Mourning and Melancholia ' (1917), *Collected Papers*, vol. iv.

them or tries to defend itself against them by the
process of repression.[1]

When it happens that a person has to give up
a sexual object, there quite often ensues a modification in his ego which can only be described as a
reinstatement of the object within the ego, as it
occurs in melancholia ; the exact nature of this
substitution is as yet unknown to us. It may be
that, by undertaking this introjection, which is a
kind of regression to the mechanism of the oral
phase, the ego makes it easier for an object to be
given up or renders that process possible. It may
even be that this identification is the sole condition
under which the id can give up its objects. At
any rate the process, especially in the early phases
of development, is a very frequent one, and it
points to the conclusion that the character of the
ego is a precipitate of abandoned object-cathexes
and that it contains a record of past object-choices.
It must, of course, be admitted from the outset

---

[1] An interesting parallel to the replacement of object-choice
by identification is to be found in the belief of primitive peoples,
and in the taboos based upon it, that the attributes of animals
which are assimilated as nourishment survive as part of the
character of the persons who eat them. As is well known, this
belief is one of the roots of cannibalism and its effects can be
traced throughout the series of customs derived from the totem
feast down to the Holy Communion. The consequences ascribed
by this belief to oral mastery of the object do in fact follow in the
case of the later sexual object-choice.

that there are varying degrees of capacity for resistance, as shown by the extent to which the character of any particular person accepts or resists the influences of the erotic object-choices through which he has lived. In women who have had many love-affairs there seems to be no difficulty in finding vestiges of their object-cathexes in the traits of their character. We must also take into consideration the case of simultaneous object-cathexis and identification, *i.e.* in which the alteration in character occurs before the object has been given up. In such a case the alteration in character would be able to survive the object-relation and in a certain sense to conserve it.

From another point of view it may be said that this transformation of an erotic object-choice into a modification of the ego is also a method by which the ego can obtain control over the id and deepen its relations with it—at the cost, it is true, of acquiescing to a large extent in the id's experiences. When the ego assumes the features of the object, it forces itself, so to speak, upon the id as a love-object and tries to make good the loss of that object by saying, 'Look, I am so like the object, you can as well love me'.

The transformation of object-libido into narcissistic libido which thus takes place obviously implies an abandonment of sexual aims, a process of desexualization ; it is consequently a kind of sublimation. Indeed, the question arises, and deserves careful consideration, whether this is not always the path taken in sublimation, whether all sublimation does not take place through the agency of the ego, which begins by changing sexual object-libido into narcissistic libido and then, perhaps, goes on to give it another aim.[1] We shall later on have to consider whether other instinctual vicissitudes may not also result from this transformation, whether, for instance, it may not bring about a defusion of the instincts that are fused together.

Although it is a digression from our theme, we cannot avoid giving our attention for a moment longer to the ego's object-identifications. If they obtain the upper hand and become too numerous, unduly intense and incompatible with one another, a pathological outcome will not be far off. It may come to a disruption of the ego in consequence of the individual identifications becoming cut off from one another by resistances ; perhaps the secret of the cases of so-called multiple personality

---

[1] Now that we have distinguished between the ego and the id, we must recognize the id as the great reservoir of libido mentioned in my introductory paper on narcissism (*Collected Papers*, vol. iv.). The libido which flows into the ego owing to the identifications described above brings about its ' secondary narcissism '.

is that the various identifications seize possession of consciousness in turn. Even when things do not go so far as this, there remains the question of conflicts between the different identifications into which the ego is split up, conflicts which cannot after all be described as purely pathological.

But, whatever the character's capacity for resisting the influences of abandoned object-cathexes may turn out to be in after years, the effects of the first identifications in earliest childhood will be profound and lasting. This leads us back to the origin of the ego-ideal ; for behind the latter there lies hidden the first and most important identification of all, the identification with the father,[1] which takes place in the prehistory of every person. This is apparently not in the first instance the consequence or outcome of an object-cathexis ; it is a direct and immediate identification and takes place earlier than any object-cathexis. But

[1] Perhaps it would be safer to say ' with the parents ' ; for before a child has arrived at definite knowledge of the difference between the sexes, the missing penis, it does not distinguish in value between its father and its mother. I recently came across the instance of a young married woman whose story showed that, after noticing the lack of a penis in herself, she had supposed it to be absent not in all women, but only in those whom she regarded as inferior, and had still supposed that her mother possessed one.

In order to simplify my presentment I shall discuss only identification with the father.

the object-choices belonging to the earliest sexual period and relating to the father and mother seem normally to find their outcome in an identification of the kind discussed, which would thus reinforce the primary one.

The whole subject, however, is so complicated that it will be necessary to go into it more minutely. The intricacy of the problem is due to two factors : the triangular character of the Oedipus situation and the constitutional bisexuality of each individual.

In its simplified form the case of the male child may be described as follows. At a very early age the little boy develops an object-cathexis of his *mother*, which originally related to the mother's breast and is the earliest instance of an object-choice on the anaclitic model ; his *father* the boy deals with by identifying himself with him. For a time these two relationships exist side by side, until the sexual wishes in regard to the mother become more intense and the father is perceived as an obstacle to them ; this gives rise to the Oedipus complex.[1] The identification with the father then takes on a hostile colouring and changes into a wish to get rid of the father in order to take his place with the mother. Henceforward the

[1] Cf. *Group Psychology and the Analysis of the Ego*, chap. vii.

relation to the father is ambivalent ; it seems as if the ambivalence inherent in the identification from the beginning had become manifest. An ambivalent attitude to the father and an object-relation of a purely affectionate kind to the mother make up the content of the simple positive Oedipus complex in the boy.

Along with the dissolution of the Oedipus complex the object-cathexis of the mother must be given up. Its place may be filled by one of two things : either an identification with the mother or an intensified identification with the father. We are accustomed to regard the latter outcome as the more normal ; it permits the affectionate relation to the mother to be in a measure retained. In this way the passing of the Oedipus complex would consolidate the masculinity in the boy's character. In a precisely analogous way, the outcome of the Oedipus attitude in the little girl may be an intensification of the identification with her mother (or such an identification may thus be set up for the first time)—a result which will stamp the child's character in the feminine mould.

These identifications are not what our previous statements would have led us to expect, since they do not involve the absorption of the abandoned object into the ego : but this alternative outcome may also occur ; it is more readily observed in girls than in boys. Analysis very often shows that a little girl, after she has had to relinquish her father as a love-object, will bring her masculinity into prominence and identify herself with her father, that is, with the object which has been lost, instead of with her mother. This will clearly depend on whether the masculinity in her disposition—whatever that may consist of—is strong enough.

It would appear, therefore, that in both sexes the relative strength of the masculine and feminine sexual dispositions is what determines whether the outcome of the Oedipus situation shall be an identification with the father or with the mother. This is one of the ways in which bisexuality takes a hand in the subsequent vicissitudes of the Oedipus complex. The other way is even more important. For one gets the impression that the simple Oedipus complex is by no means its commonest form, but rather represents a simplification or schematization which, to be sure, is often enough adequate for practical purposes. Closer study usually discloses the more complete Oedipus complex, which is twofold, positive and negative, and is due to the bisexuality originally present in children : that is to say, a boy has not merely an ambivalent attitude towards his father and an affectionate object-relation towards his mother, but at the same time he also behaves like a girl and displays an affectionate feminine attitude to his father and a corresponding hostility and jealousy towards his mother. It is this complicating element introduced by bisexuality that makes it so difficult to obtain a clear view of the facts in connection with the earliest object-choices and identifications, and still more difficult to describe them intelligibly. It may even be that the ambivalence displayed in the relations to the parents should be attributed entirely to bisexuality and that it is not, as I stated just now, developed out of an identification in consequence of rivalry.

In my opinion it is advisable in general, and quite especially where neurotics are concerned, to assume the existence of the complete Oedipus complex. Analytic experience then shows that in a number of cases one or the other of its constituents disappears, except for barely distinguishable traces, so that a series can be formed with the normal positive Oedipus complex at one end and the inverted negative one at the other, while its intermediate members will exhibit the complete type with one or other of its two constituents preponderating. As the Oedipus complex dissolves, the four trends of which it consists will group themselves in such a way as to produce a father-identification and a mother-identification. The father-identification will preserve the object-relation to the mother which belonged to the positive complex and will at the same time take the place of the object-relation to the father which belonged to the inverted complex : and the same will be true, *mutatis mutandis*, of the mother-identification. The relative intensity of the two identifications in any individual will reflect the preponderance in him of one or other of the two sexual dispositions.

The broad general outcome of the sexual phase governed by the Oedipus complex may, therefore, be taken to be the forming of a precipitate in the ego, consisting of these two identifications in some way combined together. This modification of the ego retains its special position ; it stands in contrast to the other constituents of the ego in the form of an ego-ideal or super-ego.

The super-ego is, however, not merely a deposit left by the earliest object-choices of the id ; it also represents an energetic reaction-formation against those choices. Its relation to the ego is not exhausted by the precept : ' You *ought to be* such and such (like your father) ' ; it also comprises the prohibition : ' You *must not be* such and such (like your father) ; that is, you may not do all that he does ; many things are his prerogative '. This double aspect of the ego-ideal derives from the fact that the ego-ideal had the task of effecting the repression of the Oedipus complex, indeed, it is to that revolutionary event that it owes its existence. Clearly the repression of the Oedipus complex was no easy task. The parents, and especially the father, were perceived as the obstacle to realization of the Oedipus wishes; so the child's ego brought in a reinforcement to help in carrying out the repression by erecting this same obstacle within itself. The strength to do this was, so to speak, borrowed from the father, and this loan was an extraordinarily momentous act. The super-ego retains the character of the father, while the more intense the Oedipus complex was and the more rapidly it succumbed to repression (under the influence of discipline, religious teaching, schooling and reading) the more exacting later on is the domination of the super-ego over the ego—in the form of conscience or perhaps of an unconscious sense of guilt. I shall later on bring forward a suggestion about the source of the power it employs to dominate in this way, the source, that is, of its compulsive character which manifests itself in the form of a categorical imperative.

If we consider once more the origin of the

super-ego as we have described it, we shall perceive it to be the outcome of two highly important factors, one of them biological and the other historical : namely, the lengthy duration in man of the helplessness and dependence belonging to childhood, and the fact of his Oedipus complex, the repression of which we have shown to be connected with the interruption of libidinal development by the latency period and so with the twofold onset of activity characteristic of man's sexual life.[1]   According to the view of one psycho-analyst, the last-mentioned phenomenon, which seems to be peculiar to man, is a heritage of the cultural development necessitated by the glacial epoch. We see, then, that the differentiation of the super-ego from the ego is no matter of chance ; it stands as the representative of the most important events in the development both of the individual and of the race ; indeed, by giving permanent expression to the influence of the parents it perpetuates the existence of the factors to which it owes its origin.

Psycho-analysis has been reproached time after time with ignoring the higher, moral, spiritual side of human nature. The reproach is doubly unjust,

[1] [This sentence represents a slight modification of the original text in accordance with direct instructions from the author.— TRANS.]

both historically and methodologically. For, in the first place, we have from the very beginning attributed the function of instigating repression to the moral and æsthetic tendencies in the ego, and secondly, there has been a general refusal to recognize that psycho-analytic research could not produce a complete and finished body of doctrine, like a philosophical system, ready-made, but had to find its way step by step along the path towards understanding the intricacies of the mind by making an analytic dissection of both normal and abnormal phenomena. So long as the study of the repressed part of the mind was our task, there was no need for us to feel any agitated apprehensions about the existence of the higher side of mental life. But now that we have embarked upon the analysis of the ego we can give an answer to all those whose moral sense has been shocked and who have complained that there must surely be a higher nature in man : ' Very true,' we can say, ' and here we have that higher nature, in this ego-ideal or super-ego, the representative of our relation to our parents. When we were little children we knew these higher natures, we admired them and feared them ; and later we took them into ourselves.'

The ego-ideal, therefore, is the heir of the

Oedipus complex and thus it is also the expression of the most powerful impulses and most important vicissitudes experienced by the libido in the id. By setting up this ego-ideal the ego masters its Oedipus complex and at the same time places itself in subjection to the id. Whereas the ego is essentially the representative of the external world, of reality, the super-ego stands in contrast to it as the representative of the internal world, of the id. Conflicts between the ego and the ideal will, as we are now prepared to find, ultimately reflect the contrast between what is real and what is mental, between the external world and the internal world.

Through the forming of the ideal, all the traces left behind in the id by biological developments and by the vicissitudes gone through by the human race are taken over by the ego and lived through again by it in each individual. Owing to the way in which it is formed, the ego-ideal has a great many points of contact with the phylogenetic endowment of each individual—his archaic heritage. And thus it is that what belongs to the lowest depths in the minds of each one of us is changed, through this formation of the ideal, into what we value as the highest in the human soul. It would be vain, however, to attempt to localize the ego-ideal, even in the sense in which we have localized the ego, or to work it into any of those analogies with the help of which we have tried to picture the relation between the ego and the id.

It is easy to show that the ego-ideal answers in every way to what is expected of the higher nature of man. In so far as it is a substitute for the longing for a father, it contains the germ from which all religions have evolved. The self-judgement which declares that the ego falls short of its ideal produces the sense of worthlessness with which the religious believer attests his longing. As a child grows up, the office of father is carried on by masters and by others in authority; the power of their injunctions and prohibitions remains vested in the ego-ideal and continues, in the form of conscience, to exercise the censorship of morals. The tension between the demands of conscience and the actual attainments of the ego is experienced as a sense of guilt. Social feelings rest on the foundation of identifications with others, on the basis of an ego-ideal in common with them.

Religion, morality, and a social sense—the chief elements of what is highest in man [1]—were originally one and the same thing. According to the hypothesis which I have put forward in *Totem und*

---

[1] I am at the moment putting science and art on one side.

D

Tabu they were acquired phylogenetically out of the father-complex : religion and moral restraint by the actual process of mastering the Oedipus complex itself, and social feeling from the necessity for overcoming the rivalry that then remained between the members of the younger generation. It seems that the male sex has taken the lead in developing all of these moral acquisitions ; and that they have then been transmitted to women by cross-inheritance. Even to-day the social feelings arise in the individual as a superstructure founded upon impulses of jealousy and rivalry against his brothers and sisters. Since the enmity cannot be gratified there develops an identification with the former rival. The study of mild cases of homosexuality confirms the suspicion that in this instance, too, the identification is a substitute for an affectionate object-choice which has succeeded the hostile, aggressive attitude.[1]

With the mention of phylogenesis, however, fresh problems arise, from which one is tempted to shrink back dismayed. But there is no help for it, the attempt must be made ; in spite of a fear that it will lay bare the inadequacy of the whole structure that we have so arduously built up. The

[1] Cf. *Group Psychology and the Analysis of the Ego* ; and ' Certain Neurotic Mechanisms in Jealousy, Paranoia and Homosexuality ' (1922), *Collected Papers*, vol. ii.

question is : which was it, the ego of primitive
man or his id, that acquired religion and morality
in those early days out of the father-complex ?
If it was his ego, why do we not speak simply of
these things being inherited by the ego ? If it
was the id, how does that agree with the character
of the id ? Or are we wrong in carrying the
differentiation between ego, super-ego, and id back
into such early times ? Or should we not honestly
confess that our whole conception of the processes
within the ego is of no help in understanding
phylogenesis and cannot be applied to it ?

Let us answer first what is easiest to answer.
The differentiation between ego and id must be
attributed not only to primitive man but even to
much simpler forms of life, for it is the inevitable
expression of the influence of the external world.
The super-ego, according to our hypothesis, actually
originated from the experiences that led to
totemism. The question whether it was the ego
or the id that experienced and acquired these
things soon ceases to have any meaning. Reflec-
tion at once shows us that no external vicissitudes
can be experienced or undergone by the id, except
by way of the ego, which is the representative of
the outer world to the id. Nevertheless it is not
possible to speak of direct inheritance by the ego.

It is here that the gulf between the actual individual and the conception of the species becomes evident. Moreover, one must not take the difference between ego and id in too hard-and-fast a sense, nor forget that the ego is a part of the id which has been specially modified. The experiences undergone by the ego seem at first to be lost to posterity; but, when they have been repeated often enough and with sufficient intensity in the successive individuals of many generations, they transform themselves, so to say, into experiences of the id, the impress of which is preserved by inheritance. Thus in the id, which is capable of being inherited, are stored up vestiges of the existences led by countless former egos; and, when the ego forms its super-ego out of the id, it may perhaps only be reviving images of egos that have passed away and be securing them a resurrection.

The way in which the super-ego came into being explains how it is that the earlier conflicts of the ego with the object-cathexes of the id can be carried on and continued in conflicts with their successor, the super-ego. If the ego has not succeeded in mastering the Oedipus complex satisfactorily, the energic cathexis of the latter, springing from the id, will find an outlet in the reaction-formations of the ego-ideal. The very free communication possible between the ideal and these Ucs instinctual trends explains how it is that the ideal itself can be to a great extent unconscious and inaccessible to the ego. The struggle which once raged in the deepest strata of the mind, and was not brought to an end by rapid sublimation and identification, is now carried on in a higher region, like the Battle of the Huns which in Kaulbach's painting is being fought out in the sky.

IV

THE TWO CLASSES OF INSTINCTS

W E have already said that, if the differentiation we have made of the
mind into an id, an ego, and a super-
ego represents any advance in our knowledge, it
ought to enable us to understand more thoroughly
the dynamic relations within the mind and to
describe them more clearly. We have also already
reached the conclusion that the ego is especially
affected by perception, and that, speaking broadly,
perceptions may be said to have the same significance for the ego as instincts have for the id.
At the same time the ego is subject to the influence
of the instincts, too, like the id, of which it is in
fact only a specially modified part.

I have lately developed a view of the instincts [1]
which I shall here hold to and take as the basis
of further discussions. According to this view we

[1] *Beyond the Pleasure Principle.*

54

have to distinguish two classes of instincts, one of which, Eros or the sexual instincts, is by far the more conspicuous and accessible to study. It comprises not merely the uninhibited sexual instinct proper and the impulses of a sublimated or aim-inhibited nature derived from it, but also the self-preservative instinct, which must be assigned to the ego and which at the beginning of our analytic work we had good reason for setting in opposition to the sexual object-instincts. The second class of instincts was not so easy to define ; in the end we came to recognize sadism as its representative. As a result of theoretical considerations, supported by biology, we assumed the existence of a death-instinct, the task of which is to lead organic matter back into the inorganic state ; on the other hand, we supposed that Eros aims at complicating life by bringing about a more and more far-reaching coalescence of the particles into which living matter has been dispersed, thus, of course, aiming at the maintenance of life. Acting in this way, both the instincts would be conservative in the strictest sense of the word, since both would be endeavouring to re-establish a state of things that was disturbed by the emergence of life. The appearance of life would thus be regarded as the cause of the continuance of life and also as the cause of the striving towards death; and life itself would be a conflict and compromise between these two trends. The problem of the origin of life would remain a cosmological one; and the problem of the purpose and goal of life would be answered dualistically.

On this view a special physiological process (of anabolism or katabolism) would be associated with each of the two classes of instincts; both instincts would be active in every particle of living substance, although in unequal proportions, so that some one substance might be the principal representative of Eros.

This hypothesis throws no light whatever upon the manner in which the two classes of instincts are fused, blended, and mingled with each other; but that this takes place regularly and very extensively is an assumption indispensable to our conception. It appears that, as a result of the combination of unicellular organisms into multicellular forms of life, the death-instinct of the single cell can successfully be neutralized and the destructive impulses be diverted towards the external world through the instrumentality of a special organ. This special organ would seem to be the musculature; and the death-instinct would thus seem to express itself—though probably only in part—as an instinct of destruction directed against the external world and other living organisms.

Once we have admitted the conception of a fusion of the two classes of instincts with each other, the possibility of a—more or less complete—'defusion' of them forces itself upon us. The sadistic component of the sexual instinct would be a classical example of instinctual fusion serving a useful purpose ; and the perversion in which sadism has made itself independent would be typical of defusion, though not of absolutely complete defusion. From this point we obtain a new view of a great array of facts which have not before been considered in this light. We perceive that for purposes of discharge the instinct of destruction is habitually enlisted in the service of Eros ; we suspect that the epileptic fit is a product and sign of instinctual defusion ; and we come to understand that defusion and the marked emergence of the death-instinct are among the most noteworthy effects of many severe neuroses, *e.g.* the obsessional neuroses. Making a swift generalization, we might conjecture that the essence of a regression of libido, *e.g.* from the genital to the sadistic-anal level, would lie in a defusion of instincts, just as, conversely, the advance from an earlier to the definitive genital phase would be

conditioned by an accession of erotic components.
The question also arises whether ordinary ambivalence, which is so often unusually strong in the
constitutional disposition to neurosis, should not
be regarded as the product of a defusion ; ambivalence, however, is such a fundamental phenomenon that it more probably represents a state of
incomplete fusion.

It is natural that we should now turn with
interest to inquire whether there may not be
instructive connections to be traced between the
formations we have assumed to exist in the mind
—the ego, the super-ego, and the id—and the two
classes of instincts ; and, further, whether the
pleasure-principle which dominates mental processes can be shown to have any constant relation
both to the two classes of instincts and to these
differentiations which we have drawn within the
mind. But before we discuss this, we must clear
away a doubt which arises concerning the terms
of the problem itself. There can be no doubt
about the pleasure-principle, and the differentiations within the ego have good clinical justification,
but the distinction between the two classes of
instincts does not seem sufficiently assured and it
is possible that facts of clinical analysis may be
found to conflict with it.

One such fact appears to exist. Instead of the opposition between the two classes of instincts let us consider the polarity of love and hate. (There is no difficulty in finding a representative of Eros ; but we must be grateful that we can find a representative of the elusive death-instinct in the instinct of destruction, for which hate points the way.) Now, clinical observation shows not only that love is with unexpected regularity accompanied by hate (ambivalence), and not only that in human relationships hate is frequently a forerunner of love, but also that in many circumstances hate changes into love and love into hate. If this change is anything more than a mere succession in time, then clearly the ground is cut away from under a distinction so fundamental as that between erotic instincts and death-instincts, one which presupposes the existence of physiological processes running counter to each other.

Now the case in which someone first loves and then hates the same person (or the reverse), because that person has given him cause for doing so, has obviously nothing to do with our problem. Nor has the other case in which feelings of love that have not yet become manifest express themselves to begin with by enmity and aggressive tendencies ; for it may be that here the destructive components

in the object-cathexis have outstripped the erotic
and are only later on joined by the latter. But
we know of several instances in the psychology of
the neuroses in which there are better grounds for
assuming that a transformation does take place.
In persecutory paranoia the sufferer takes a
particular way of defending himself against an
unduly strong homosexual attachment to a given
person, with the result that the person he once
loved most is changed into a persecutor and then
becomes the object of aggressive and often dangerous impulses on the part of the patient. Here
we have grounds for interposing an intermediate
phase in which the love is transformed into hate.
Analytic investigation has only lately revealed
that the sources of homosexuality and of desexualized social feelings include very intense feelings of rivalry giving rise to aggressive desires,
which, after they have been surmounted, are
succeeded by love for the object that was formerly
hated or by an identification with it. The question
arises whether in these instances we are to assume
a direct transformation of hate into love. It is
clear that here the changes are purely internal and
an alteration in the behaviour of the object plays
no part in them.

There is another possible mechanism, however,

which we have come to know of by analytic investigation of the processes concerned in the change in paranoia. An ambivalent attitude is present from the outset and the transformation is effected by means of a reactive shifting of cathexis, by which energy is withdrawn from the erotic impulses and used to supplement the hostile energy.

Not quite the same thing but something like it happens when a hostile attitude of rivalry is overcome and leads to homosexuality. The hostile attitude has no prospect of gratification; consequently—*i.e.* as an economic measure—it is replaced by a loving attitude for which there is more hope of satisfaction, that is, possibility of discharge. So we see that we are not obliged in either of these cases to assume a direct transformation of hate into love which would be incompatible with a qualitative distinction between the two classes of instincts.

It appears, however, that by including in our calculations this other mechanism by means of which love can be changed into hate, we have tacitly made another assumption which deserves to be formulated explicitly. We have reckoned as though there existed in the mind—whether in the ego or in the id—a displaceable energy, which is in itself neutral, but is able to join forces either with an erotic or with a destructive impulse, differing qualitatively as they do, and augment its total cathexis. Without assuming the existence of a displaceable energy of this kind we can make no headway. The only question is where it comes from, what it belongs to, and what it signifies.

The problem of the quality of instinctual impulses and of its persistence throughout their vicissitudes is still very obscure and has hardly been attacked up to the present. In the sexual component-instincts, which are especially accessible to observation, it is possible to perceive the working of processes which are in the same category as what we are discussing ; *e.g.* we see that some degree of communication exists between the component instincts, that an instinct deriving from one particular erotogenic source can make over its intensity to reinforce another component-instinct originating in another source, that gratification of one instinct can take the place of gratification of another, and many more facts of the same nature —all of which must encourage us to venture upon certain assumptions.

In the present discussion, moreover, I am putting forward nothing but a supposition ; I have no proof to offer. It seems a plausible view that this neutral displaceable energy, which is probably active alike in the ego and in the id, proceeds from the narcissistic reservoir of libido, *i.e.* that it is desexualized Eros. (The erotic instincts appear to be altogether more plastic, more readily diverted and displaced than the destructive instincts.) From this we can easily go on to assume that this displaceable libido is employed in the service of the pleasure-principle to obviate accumulations and to facilitate discharge. It is clear, incidentally, that there is a certain indifference about the path along which the discharge takes place, so long as it takes place somehow. We know this trait; it is characteristic of the cathectic processes in the id. It is found in erotic cathexes, where a peculiar indifference in regard to the object displays itself; and it is especially evident in the transferences arising in analysis, which develop inevitably no matter who the analyst may be. Rank has recently published some good examples of the way in which neurotic acts of revenge can be directed against the wrong people. Such behaviour on the part of the unconscious reminds one of the comic story of the three village tailors, one of whom had to be hanged because the only village blacksmith had committed a capital offence. The penalty must be exacted even if it does not fall upon the guilty.

It was in studying dream-work that we first came
upon this kind of looseness in the displacements
brought about by the primary process. In that
case it was the objects that were thus relegated to
a position of no more than secondary importance,
just as in the case we are now discussing it is the
paths of discharge. It would seem to be characteristic of the ego to be more particular both
about the choice of an object and about the path
of discharge.

If this displaceable energy is desexualized libido,
it might also be described as sublimated energy ;
for it would still retain the main purpose of Eros
—that of uniting and binding—in so far as it
helped towards establishing that unity, or tendency
to unity, which is particularly characteristic of the
ego. If the intellectual processes in the wider
sense are to be classed among these displacements,
then the energy for the work of thought itself
must be supplied from sublimated erotic sources.

Here we arrive again at the possibility which
has already been discussed that sublimation may
take place regularly through the mediation of the
ego. The other case will be recollected, in which
the ego deals with the first object-cathexes of the
id (and certainly with later ones too) by taking
over the libido from them into itself and binding

it to the ego-modification produced by means of identification. The transformation of erotic libido into ego-libido of course involves an abandonment of sexual aims, a desexualization. In any case this throws light upon an important function of the ego in its relation to Eros. By thus obtaining possession of the libido from the object-cathexes, setting itself up as sole love-object, and desexualizing or sublimating the libido of the id, the ego is working in opposition to the purposes of Eros and placing itself at the service of the opposing instinctual trends. It has to acquiesce in some of the other object-cathexes of the id; it has to go hand in hand with them, so to speak. We shall come back later to another possible consequence of this activity of the ego.

This would seem to imply an important amplification of the theory of narcissism. At the very beginning all the libido is accumulated in the id, while the ego is still in process of formation or far from robust. Part of this libido is sent out by the id into erotic object-cathexes, whereupon the ego, now growing stronger, attempts to obtain possession of this object-libido and to force itself upon the id as a love-object. The narcissism of the ego is thus seen to be secondary, acquired by the withdrawal of the libido from objects.

E

Over and over again we find on tracing instinct-ual impulses back that they disclose themselves as derivatives of Eros. If it were not for the considerations put forward in *Beyond the Pleasure Principle*, and ultimately for the sadistic con-stituents which have attached themselves to Eros, we should have difficulty in holding to our funda-mental dualistic point of view. But since we cannot escape that view, we are driven to conclude that the death-instincts are by their nature mute and that the clamour of life proceeds for the most part from Eros.[1]

And from the struggle against Eros! It can hardly be doubted that the pleasure-principle serves the id as a compass in its struggle against the libido—the force that introduces such disturb-ances into the process of life. If it is true that life is governed by Fechner's principle of constant equilibrium, it consists of a continuous descent towards death; but the falling of the level is delayed and fresh tensions are introduced by the claims of Eros, of the sexual instincts, as expressed in instinctual needs. The id, guided by the pleasure-principle, that is, by the perception of 'pain', guards itself against these tensions in

[1] In fact, according to our view it is through the agency of Eros that the destructive instincts that are directed towards the external world have been diverted from the self.

various ways. It does so in the first place by complying as swiftly as possible with the demands of the non-desexualized libido, *i.e.* by striving for the gratification of the directly sexual trends. But it does so further, and in a far more comprehensive fashion, in relation to one particular form of gratification which subsumes all component claims—that is, by discharge of the sexual substances, which are saturated conductors, so to speak, of the erotic tensions. The ejection of sexual substances in the sexual act corresponds in a certain degree with the separation of soma and germ-plasm. This accounts for the likeness between dying and the condition that follows complete sexual satisfaction, and for the fact that death coincides with the act of copulation in some of the lower animals. These creatures die in the act of reproduction because, after Eros has been eliminated through the process of gratification, the death-instinct has a free hand for accomplishing its purposes. Finally, as we have seen, the ego, by sublimating some of the libido for itself and its purposes, assists the id in its work of mastering the tensions.

V

THE SUBORDINATE RELATIONSHIPS
OF THE EGO

THE complexity of our subject-matter must be an excuse for the fact that none of the chapter-headings of this book correspond entirely to their contents, and that in turning to new aspects of the problem we constantly hark back to matters that have already been dealt with.

As has been said repeatedly, the ego is formed to a great extent out of identifications taking the place of cathexes on the part of the id which have been abandoned ; the earliest of these identifications always fulfil a special office in the ego and stand apart from the rest of the ego in the form of a super-ego, while later on, as it grows stronger, the ego may become more able to withstand the effects of identifications. The super-ego owes its special position in the ego, or in regard to the ego, to a factor which must be considered from two sides : to the fact that on the one hand it was the first identification and one which took place while the ego was still feeble, and that on the other hand it was the heir to the Oedipus complex and thus incorporated into the ego objects of far greater significance than any others. The super-ego's relation to the subsequent modifications effected in the ego is roughly that of the primary sexual period in childhood to full-grown sexual activity after puberty. Although it is amenable to every later influence, it preserves throughout life the character given to it by its derivation from the father-complex, namely, the capacity to stand apart from the ego and to rule it. It is a memorial of the former weakness and dependence of the ego and the mature ego remains subject to its domination. As the child was once compelled to obey its parents, so the ego submits to the categorical imperative pronounced by its super-ego.

The descent of the super-ego from the first object-cathexes of the id, from the Oedipus complex, however, signifies even more for it. This descent, as we have already described, connects it with the phylogenetic acquisitions of the id and makes it a reincarnation of former ego-structures which have left their precipitates behind in the id. Thus the super-ego is always in close touch with

the id and can act as its representative in relation
to the ego.   It reaches deep down into the id and
is for that reason farther from consciousness than
the ego.[1]

We can best appreciate these relations by turning our attention to certain clinical facts, which
have long since lost their novelty but which still
await theoretical discussion.

There are certain people who behave in a quite
peculiar fashion during the work of analysis.
When one speaks hopefully to them or expresses
satisfaction with the progress of the treatment,
they show signs of discontent and their condition
invariably becomes worse.   One begins by regarding this as defiance and as an attempt to prove
their superiority to the physician, but later one
comes to take a deeper and truer view.   One
becomes convinced, not only that such people
cannot endure any praise or appreciation, but that
they react inversely to the progress of the treatment.   Every partial solution that ought to result,
and in other people does result, in an improvement
or a temporary suspension of symptoms produces
in them for the time being an exacerbation of their
illness ; they get worse during the treatment

[1] It may be said that the psycho-analytical or metapsychological ego stands on its head no less than the anatomical ego—
the ' cortical homunculus '.

instead of getting better. They exhibit the so-called negative therapeutic reaction.

There is no doubt that there is something in these people that sets itself against their recovery and dreads its approach as though it were a danger. We are accustomed to say that the need for illness has got the upper hand in them over the desire for health. If we analyse this resistance in the usual way—then, even after we have subtracted from it the defiant attitude towards the physician and the fixation on the various kinds of advantage which the patient derives from the illness, the greater part of it is still left over; and this reveals itself as the most powerful of all obstacles to recovery, more powerful even than such familiar ones as narcissistic inaccessibility, the assumption of a negative attitude towards the physician or a clinging to the advantages of the illness.

In the end we come to see that we are dealing with what may be called a ' moral ' factor, a sense of guilt, which is finding atonement in the illness and is refusing to give up the penalty of suffering. We are justified in regarding this rather disheartening explanation as conclusive. But as far as the patient is concerned this sense of guilt is dumb; it does not tell him he is guilty; he does not feel guilty, he simply feels ill. This sense of guilt expresses itself only as a resistance to recovery which it is extremely difficult to overcome. It is also particularly difficult to convince the patient that this motive lies behind his continuing to be ill ; he holds fast to the more obvious explanation that treatment by analysis is not the right remedy for his case.[1]

The description we have given applies to the most extreme instances of this state of affairs, but

[1] The battle with the obstacle of an unconscious sense of guilt is not made easy for the analyst. Nothing can be done against it directly, and nothing indirectly but the slow procedure of unmasking its unconscious repressed roots, and of thus gradually changing it into a conscious sense of guilt. One has a special opportunity for influencing it when this Ucs sense of guilt is a ' borrowed ' one, *i.e.* when it is the product of an identification with some other person who was once the object of an erotic cathexis. When the sense of guilt has been adopted in this way it is often the sole remaining trace of the abandoned love-relation and not at all easy to recognize as such. (The likeness between this process and what happens in melancholia is unmistakable.) If one can unmask this former object-cathexis behind the Ucs sense of guilt, the therapeutic success is often brilliant, but otherwise the outcome of one's efforts is by no means certain. It depends principally on the intensity of the sense of guilt ; there is often no counteracting force of similar strength which the treatment can put in motion against it. Perhaps it may depend, too, on whether the personality of the analyst allows of the patient's putting him in the place of his ego-ideal, and this involves a temptation for the analyst to play the part of prophet, saviour, and redeemer to the patient. Since the rules of analysis are diametrically opposed to the physician's making use of his personality in any such manner, it must be honestly confessed that here we have another limitation to the effectiveness of analysis ; after all, analysis does not set out to abolish the possibility of morbid reactions, but to give the patient's ego *freedom* to choose one way or the other.

in a lesser measure this factor has to be reckoned with in very many cases, perhaps in all severe cases of neurosis.   In fact it may be precisely this element in the situation, the attitude of the ego-ideal, that determines the severity of a neurotic illness.   We shall not hesitate, therefore, to discuss rather more fully the way in which the sense of guilt expresses itself under different conditions.

An explanation of the normal conscious sense of guilt (conscience) presents no difficulties ; it is due to tension between the ego and the ego-ideal and is the expression of a condemnation of the ego pronounced by its criticizing function.   The feelings of inferiority so well known in neurotics are presumably closely related to it.   In two very familiar maladies the sense of guilt is over-strongly conscious ; in them the ego-ideal displays particular severity and often rages against the ego with the utmost cruelty.   The attitude of the ego-ideal in these two diseases, the obsessional neurosis and melancholia, presents, alongside of this similarity, differences that are no less significant.

In certain forms of the obsessional neurosis the sense of guilt expresses itself loudly but cannot justify itself to the ego. Consequently the patient's ego rebels against this imputation of guilt and seeks the physician's support in repudiating it.   It would be folly to acquiesce in this, for to do so would have no effect. Analysis shows that the super-ego is being influenced by processes that have remained hidden from the ego. It is possible to discover the repressed impulses which really occasion the sense of guilt. The super-ego is thus proved to have known more than the ego about the unconscious id.

In melancholia the impression that the super-ego has obtained a hold upon consciousness is even stronger. But in this case the ego ventures no objection ; it admits the guilt and submits to the punishment. The explanation of this difference is plain. In the obsessional neurosis the reprehensible impulses which are being criticized by the super-ego have never formed part of the ego, while in melancholia the object of the super-ego's wrath has become part of the ego through identification.

It is certainly not clear why the sense of guilt reaches such an extraordinary intensity in these two neurotic disorders ; and indeed, the main problem presented in this state of affairs lies in another direction. We shall postpone discussion of it until we have dealt with the other cases—in which the sense of guilt remains unconscious.

It is essentially in hysteria and in states of a hysterical type that this condition is found. The

mechanism by which the sense of guilt is kept unconscious is easy to discover. The hysterical type
of ego defends itself from the painful perception
which the criticisms of its super-ego threaten to
produce in it by the same means that it uses to
defend itself from an unendurable object-cathexis—
by an act of repression. It is the ego, therefore,
that is responsible for the sense of guilt remaining
unconscious. We know that as a rule the ego
carries out repressions in the service and at the
behest of its super-ego ; but this is a case in which
it has turned the same weapon against its harsh
taskmaster. In the obsessional neurosis, as we
know, the phenomena of reaction-formation pre-
dominate ; but here the ego contents itself with
keeping at a distance the material to which the
sense of guilt refers.

One may go further and venture the hypothesis
that a great part of the sense of guilt must normally
remain unconscious, because the origin of conscience is closely connected with the Oedipus complex which belongs to the unconscious. If any
one were inclined to put forward the paradoxical
proposition that the normal man is not only far
more immoral than he believes but also far more
moral than he has any idea of, psycho-analysis,
which is responsible for the first half of the asser-

tion, would have no objection to raise against the second half.[1]

It was a surprise to find that exacerbation of this Ucs sense of guilt could turn people into criminals. But it is undoubtedly a fact. In many criminals, especially youthful ones, it is possible to detect a very powerful sense of guilt which existed before the crime, and is not therefore the result of it but its motive. It is as if it had been a relief to be able to fasten this unconscious sense of guilt on to something real and immediate.

In all these situations the super-ego displays its independence of the conscious ego and the closeness of its relations with the unconscious id. And now, having regard to the importance we ascribed to preconscious verbal residues in the ego, the question arises whether the super-ego, if it is in part unconscious, can consist in such verbal images, or, if not, in what it does consist. Our answer, though it does not carry us very far, will be that it cannot possibly be disputed that the super-ego, no less than the ego, is derived from auditory impressions ; it is part of the ego and remains to a great extent accessible to consciousness by way

[1] This proposition is only apparently a paradox ; it simply states that human nature has a far greater capacity, both for good and for evil, than it thinks it has, i.e. than it is aware of through the conscious perceptions of the ego.

of these verbal images (concepts, abstractions), but the cathectic energy of these elements of the super-ego does not originate from the auditory perceptions, instruction, reading, etc., but from sources in the id.

The question which we postponed answering runs thus : How is it that the super-ego manifests itself essentially as a sense of guilt (or rather, as criticism—for the sense of guilt is the perception in the ego which corresponds to the criticism) and at the same time develops such extraordinary harshness and severity towards the ego ? If we turn to melancholia first, we find that the excessively strong super-ego which has obtained a hold upon consciousness rages against the ego with merciless fury, as if it had taken possession of the whole of the sadism available in the person concerned. Following our view of sadism, we should say that the destructive component had entrenched itself in the super-ego and turned against the ego. What is now holding sway in the super-ego is, as it were, a pure culture of the death-instinct, and in fact it often enough succeeds in driving the ego into death, if the latter does not protect itself from the tyrant in time by a revulsion into mania.

The reproaches of conscience in certain forms of obsessional neurosis are just as painful and

tormenting, but here the situation is less perspicuous. It is remarkable that the obsessional
neurotic, in contrast to the melancholiac, never
takes the step of self-destruction ; he is as if
immune against the danger of suicide, and is far
better protected from it than the hysteric. We
can see that what guarantees the safety of the ego
is the fact that the object has been retained. In
the obsessional neurosis it has become possible,
through a regression to the pre-genital organization, for the love-impulses to transform themselves
into impulses of aggression against the object.
Here again the instinct of destruction has been set
free and it aims at destroying the object, or at
least it appears to have this aim. These tendencies have not been adopted by the ego ; it
struggles against them with reaction-formations
and precautionary measures, and they remain in
the id. The super-ego, however, behaves as if the
ego were responsible for them and shows by its
zeal in chastising these destructive intentions that
they are no mere semblance evoked by regression
but an actual substitution of hate for love. Help-
less in either direction, the ego defends itself vainly,
alike against the instigations of the murderous id
and against the reproaches of the punishing conscience. It succeeds in holding in check at least

the most brutal actions of both sides ; the first outcome is interminable self-torment, and eventually there follows a systematic torturing of the object, in so far as it is within reach.

The activity of the dangerous death-instincts within the individual organism is dealt with in various ways ; in part they are rendered harmless by being fused with erotic components, in part they are diverted towards the external world in the form of aggression, while for the most part they undoubtedly continue their inner work unhindered. How is it then that in melancholia the super-ego can become a kind of gathering-place for the death-instincts ?

From the point of view of morality, the control and restriction of instinct, it may be said of the id that it is totally non-moral, of the ego that it strives to be moral, and of the super-ego that it can be hyper-moral and then becomes as ruthless as only the id can be. It is remarkable that the more a man checks his aggressive tendencies towards others the more tyrannical, that is aggressive, he becomes in his ego-ideal. The ordinary view sees the situation the other way round : the standard set up by the ego-ideal seems to be the motive for the suppression of aggressiveness. The fact remains, however, as we have stated it : the more a man controls his aggressiveness, the more intense become the aggressive tendencies of his ego-ideal against his ego. It is like a displacement, a turning round upon the self. But even ordinary normal morality has a harshly restraining, cruelly prohibiting quality. It is from this, indeed, that the conception arises of an inexorable higher being who metes out punishment.

I cannot go further in my consideration of these questions without introducing a fresh assumption. The super-ego arises, as we know, from an identification with the father regarded as a model. Every such identification is in the nature of a de-sexualization or even of a sublimation. It now seems as though when a transformation of this kind takes place there occurs at the same time an instinctual defusion. After sublimation the erotic component no longer has the power to bind the whole of the destructive elements that were previously combined with it, and these are released in the form of inclinations to aggression and destruction. This defusion would be the source of the general character of harshness and cruelty exhibited by the ideal—its dictatorial 'Thou shalt'.

Let us again consider the obsessional neurosis for a moment. The state of affairs is different here. The defusion of love into aggressiveness has not been effected by the agency of the ego, but is the result of a regression which has come about in the id. But this process has extended beyond the id to the super-ego, which now increases its tyranny over the innocent ego. It would seem, however, that in this case no less than in that of melancholia, the ego, having gained possession of the libido by means of identification, is punished for doing so by the super-ego through the instrumentality of the aggressiveness which had before been mixed with the libido.

Our ideas about the ego are beginning to clear, and its various relationships are gaining distinctness. We now see the ego in its strength and in its weaknesses. It is entrusted with important functions. By virtue of its relation to the perceptual system it arranges the processes of the mind in a temporal order and tests their correspondence with reality. By interposing the process of thinking it secures a postponement of motor discharges and controls the avenues to motility. This last office is, to be sure, a question more of form than of fact; in the matter of action the ego's position is like that of a constitutional monarch, without whose sanction no law can be passed but who hesitates long before imposing a veto on any measure put forward by Parliament.

F

All the experiences of life that originate from without enrich the ego; the id, however, is another outer world to it, which it strives to bring into subjection to itself. It withdraws libido from the id and transforms the object-cathexes of the id into ego-constructions. With the aid of the super-ego, though in a manner that is still obscure to us, it draws upon the experiences of past ages stored in the id.

There are two paths by which the contents of the id can penetrate into the ego. The one is direct, the other leads by way of the ego-ideal; which of these two paths they take may, for many mental activities, be of decisive importance. The ego develops from perceiving instincts to controlling them, from obeying instincts to curbing them. In this achievement a large share is taken by the ego-ideal, which indeed is partly a reaction-formation against the instinctual processes in the id. Psycho-analysis is an instrument to enable the ego to push its conquest of the id further still.

From the other point of view, however, we see this same ego as a poor creature owing service to three masters and consequently menaced by three several dangers: from the external world, from the libido of the id, and from the severity of the super-ego. Three kinds of anxiety correspond to these three dangers, since anxiety is the expression of a recoil from danger. Like the dweller in a borderland that it is, the ego tries to mediate between the world and the id, to make the id comply with the world's demands and, by means of muscular activity, to accommodate the world to the id's desires. In point of fact it behaves like the physician during treatment by analysis; it offers itself to the id as a libidinal object in view of its power of adaptation to the real world, and aims at attaching the id's libido to itself. It is not only the ally of the id; it is also a submissive slave who courts the love of his master. Whenever possible, it tries to remain on good terms with the id; it draws the veil of its Pcs rationalizations over the id's Ucs demands; it pretends that the id is showing obedience to the mandates of reality, even when in fact it is remaining obdurate and immovable; it throws a disguise over the id's conflicts with reality and, if possible, over its conflicts with the super-ego too. Its position midway between the id and reality tempts it only too often to become sycophantic, opportunist and false, like a politician who sees the truth but wants to keep his place in popular favour.

Towards the two classes of instincts the ego's attitude is not impartial. Its work of identification and sublimation gives the death-instincts in the id assistance in mastering the libido, but in so doing it incurs the risk of itself becoming the object of the death-instincts and of perishing. In order to be able to help in this way it has to become flooded with libido itself ; it thus becomes the representative of Eros and thenceforward desires to live and to be loved.

But since the ego's work of sublimation results in a defusion of the instincts and a liberation of the aggressive instincts in the super-ego, its struggle against the libido exposes it to the danger of mal-treatment and death. In suffering under the attacks of the super-ego or perhaps even succumbing to them, the ego is meeting with a fate like that of the protozoa which are destroyed by the products of disintegration that they themselves have created. From the economic point of view the morality that functions in the super-ego seems to be a similar product of disintegration.

Among the subordinate relationships in which the ego stands, that to the super-ego is perhaps the most interesting.

The ego is the true abode of anxiety.[1] Threatened by dangers from three directions, it

---

[1] [The author's views upon anxiety as given in the following paragraphs have been largely revised in his later work, *Hemmung, Symptom und Angst.*—TRANS.]

develops the flight-reflex by withdrawing its own cathexis from the menacing perception or from the equally dreaded process in the id, and discharging it as anxiety. This primitive reaction is later replaced by the introduction of protective cathexes (the mechanism of the phobias). What it is that the ego fears either from an external or from a libidinal danger cannot be specified ; we know that it is in the nature of an overthrow or of extinction, but it is not determined by analysis. The ego is simply obeying the warning of the pleasure-principle. On the other hand, we can tell what lies hidden behind the ego's dread of the super-ego, its fear of conscience. The higher being which later became the ego-ideal once threatened the ego with castration, and this dread of castration is probably the kernel round which the subsequent fear of conscience has gathered ; it is this dread that persists as the fear of conscience.

The high-sounding phrase, ' Every fear is ultimately the fear of death ', has hardly any meaning ; at any rate it cannot be justified. It seems to me, on the contrary, perfectly correct to distinguish the fear of death from dread of an external object (objective anxiety) and from neurotic libidinal anxiety. It presents a difficult problem to psychoanalysis, for death is an abstract concept with a negative content for which no unconscious correlative can be found. It would seem that the mechanism of the fear of death can only be that the ego relinquishes its narcissistic libidinal cathexis in a very large measure, that is, that it gives up itself, just as it gives up some *external* object in other cases in which it feels anxiety. I believe that the fear of death concerns an interplay between the ego and the super-ego.

We know that the fear of death makes its appearance under two conditions (which, moreover, are entirely analogous to the other situations in which anxiety develops), namely, as a reaction to an external danger and as an internal process, as for instance in melancholia. Once again a neurotic manifestation may help us to understand a normal one.

The fear of death in melancholia only admits of one explanation : that the ego gives itself up because it feels itself hated and persecuted by the super-ego, instead of loved. To the ego, therefore, living means the same as being loved—being loved by the super-ego, which here again appears as the representative of the id. The super-ego fulfils the same function of protecting and saving that was fulfilled in earlier days by the father and later by Providence or destiny. But, when the ego finds itself in overwhelming danger of a real order which it believes itself unable to overcome by its own strength, it is bound to draw the same conclusion. It sees itself deserted by all the forces of protection and lets itself die. Here, moreover, is once again the same situation as that which underlay the first great anxiety-state of birth and the infantile anxiety of longing for an absent person —the anxiety of separation from the protecting mother.

These considerations enable us to conceive of the fear of death, like the fear of conscience, as a development of the fear of castration. The great significance which the sense of guilt has in the neuroses makes it conceivable that ordinary neurotic anxiety is reinforced in severe cases by a development of anxiety between the ego and the super-ego (fear of castration, of conscience, of death).

The id, to which we finally come back, has no means of showing the ego either love or hate. It cannot say what it wants ; it has achieved no unity of will. Eros and the death-instinct struggle within it ; we have seen with what weapons the one group of instincts defends itself against the other. It would be possible to picture the id as under the domination of the mute but powerful death-instincts, which desire to be at peace and (as the pleasure-principle demands) to put Eros, the intruder, to rest ; but that would be to run the risk of valuing too cheaply the part played by Eros.